SHA

The Adam Fender family; the author's mother is second from the right.

Shake My Hand

A Personal Touch With The Past

By

Louisa M. Burger

Illustrations by
Matt Beebe

FLOATING ISLAND PUBLICATIONS
POINT REYES STATION
1990

ISBN: 0-912449-36-5

Second Printing

Published by:

Floating Island Publications
P.O. Box 516
Point Reyes Station, California 94956

The author wishes to acknowledge Bobbie Stumpf,
Thomas Centolella, Vera Beebe, Glenn Beebe,
Thelma Johnson, Liz Schott, the Creative Writing
Class at the College of Marin, Lynn Follette,
Michael Sykes, and Billie Wood for their assistance
and encouragement in the publication of this book.

Dedicated To
All Fifth Graders
Wherever They Are

CONTENTS

Shake My Hand

SHAKE MY HAND. SHAKE IT FIRMLY.
You have shaken the hand that shook the hand that shook the hand of Abraham Lincoln.

My grandfather was born and raised in Ohio. When the Civil War broke out he signed up in Putnam County, Ohio, to serve in the Union Army, Company K, 185th Regiment, Ohio Volunteer Infantry. This was February 24, 1865. He was 20 years old.

He left for active duty almost immediately. He was in an encampment that was protecting the Capital and surrounding area.

The southern troops had gotten so close that the campfires could be seen from the Capitol steps. President Lincoln was very worried.

Having been stationed here my grandfather was seeing active duty. In a short time he received a bad wound to his leg. He was taken to a hospital that had been set up near the Capitol. President Lincoln often came in to see the troops and visit with the wounded.

One day my grandfather looked up and there at the foot of his cot stood President Lincoln.

My grandfather was so startled, he held his breath.

"Mr. Lincoln?" he whispered awefully.

"Yes," Mr. Lincoln replied as he moved over beside the cot and looked down with very sad and compassionate eyes. "I am sorry you are wounded. Are you getting good care? Is there anything I can do? Can they save your leg?"

"They think so," my grandfather said. "It looks very hopeful. Thank you so much for stopping by and showing concern for all of us."

"How long do you think you will be here?" asked Mr. Lincoln.

"Not very long now," answered my grandfather. "I want to return to my home in Ohio. I want to get some homestead land in Michigan and start clearing it for farming."

Mr. Lincoln nodded his head and reaching down, picked up my grandfather's hand and shook it firmly.

"I wish you the best in your new venture and home. I hope your leg heals enough so you can carry on your work."

With this he walked slowly to the next cot where he paused to visit with another wounded soldier.

That's how you got to shake the hand that shook the hand that shook the hand of Abraham Lincoln.

Homesteading

AFTER MY GRANDFATHER WAS WOUNDED FIGHTING WITH the troops around the Capitol, he returned to his home in Ohio to recuperate.

He was mustered out June 29, 1865 with an honorable discharge by Order of the War Department from the hospital at Louisville, Kentucky.

Although his leg healed, he suffered great pain from it the rest of his life. However, he did not let that stop him from carrying out the plans he told President Lincoln about.

He returned home to Ohio to live with his father but did not stay there long. His father decided to come to Michigan in 1865 to Barry County, where he had purchased a farm.

My grandfather came with him and helped him establish his farm. He worked there until March 1871. At that time his father died. Meanwhile, the Homestead Act had been passed so lands in the West were available to settlers without payment.

He decided then to move to Ionia County, where he had received some of this homestead land. He was now 27 years old.

This land proved to be fertile and he became a successful farmer.

However, it was completely covered with trees. If he wished to till any ground, he would have to clear the land. This was slow and arduous work for a man alone, especially crippled as he was.

He built a temporary lean-to to live in while he cleared a space big enough to put up a log cabin. The logs he cut down would be used for building.

Meanwhile, other homesteaders had moved in. They were very neighborly. They helped each other.

The men came over and helped erect the cabin. The logs were placed side by side. They were caulked in between with a mixture of clay and mud. This helped to seal the spaces between the logs.

It was not entirely successful because I can remember my mother telling that she often woke up in the morning to have drifts of snow across her bed.

It was really a spacious cabin. It contained a large living room with eating and cooking areas. A fireplace was at one end of the cabin. This served to heat the cabin and for cooking.

There were two bedrooms down and two bedrooms up with a stairway.

This was a spacious cabin compared to what most pioneers built. It was a good thing because eight children were born to them. My mother was the only girl that lived. Infant deaths were very high in those days for various reasons.

The cabin had several windows which was also unusual. It was easier to heat a cabin with few windows. It was almost impossible to make them wind and weather proof.

After the cabin was ready, my grandfather married my grandmother, Louisa, June 9th, 1874. They moved into the cabin, where they sat up housekeeping and established their home.

My grandfather was an excellent farmer and his affairs prospered.

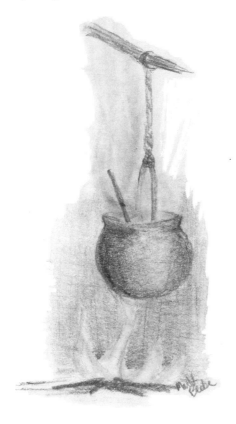

Grandpa's Smokehouse

BY 1915 MY GRANDFATHER, AS IT SAID IN THE IONIA County Records, was able to erect a "new and much more comfortable and commodious home on his place."

My sister and I often went by the smokehouse on the way to the log cabin to play. It was very pleasant to savor the delicious smells. We often turned and walked back and forth in front of it to sniff and sniff and sniff.

In 1876 my grandfather had built a small building about 60 feet from the cabin. It had a tall chimney so it could draw a good draft. There were no windows. The door was rather small.

On the door, at the lower edge, was a round hole about 5 inches across. This was covered by a moveable piece of tin or wood. They opened it if they wanted a draft.

The fire inside was usually right on the dirt floor with pieces of hickory wood stacked up. This smoldered slowly. The excess smoke came out from holes near the roof and the tall chimney.

Grandpa's smokehouse was made of wood but other materials were used. A block house was adequate. Sod houses could be built with vents in the top. This was good for smoking but not for storing.

It was built close to the cabin so my grandmother could keep an eye on it. Much of their food was in there. So many highwaymen were dropping by. They sometimes helped themselves to things.

Many of the animals liked the smell of the goodies even if they could not get in. That does not mean they did not try. Grandma said she often saw animal tracks around the building.

Special visitors were the black bears. They were mainly vegetarians, but they also dined on mice, voles and chipmunks. Although insects formed an important part of their diet, they were still interested in the smoked meats. Not only did Grandma see their tracks but splintered wood where they tried to get in. She saw raccoon tracks, too. I am sure they were more curious than hungry. Opossum tracks were hard to tell from raccoon. Even woodchuck and porcupine were interested on occasion.

The most numerous tracks were those from bobcat, red fox, coyote and timber wolves, who roamed the woods in this area.

Grandpa had started to raise pigs as soon as the cabin was finished. He got a couple of young shoats from another homesteader. He had to keep track of them, so he built a pig sty close to the cabin.

Because there was no refrigeration, when a pig

was butchered, he needed to smoke or salt down the meat to keep it.

In smoking, he used hickory wood for curing. It was available on his farm. Grandma salted some of the meat down in big crocks of lard. She called this salt pork.

If she wished to use it she freshened it up by soaking it in water before cooking. Oh, how good thick slabs of salt pork were when they were drenched in flour and fried crisp in an iron skillet in the fireplace, or later on the wood stove!

The smoking was a slow process. The hams, bacons, sausages, et cetera, were left in the smokehouse many weeks sometimes. This was the natural smoke cure. Today, most hams are artificially cured.

The smokehouse also served as a place to store meats after they were cured. Whenever they wanted anything they just went out to the smokehouse to get it. There were no stores to go to for food. With the large family they had, a ham did not last very long.

Grandpa made all his sausages. They made up two kinds. Grandma made some bulk sausage. Grandpa hand stuffed casings with his sausage mix. Most of these were also smoked.

The building stood for many years even after I graduated from college and began teaching. It was destroyed by fire around 1948. It had stood 75 years.

I felt sad. Another memory of my childhood was gone.

A Sweet Tooth

IN THE SPRING OF 1872 MY GRANDFATHER MOVED TO IONIA County, Michigan, where he settled on a homestead farm obtained from the government.

He cleared enough land to erect on that place a log cabin. In 1874, he married my grandmother, Louisa.

They set up housekeeping and made their home there.

They could raise most of what they wanted to eat. But there were some staples they needed from the nearest store in Ionia. Among these articles were salt, pepper, tea, coffee, sugar and flour. They also needed to buy most of their clothing and shoes.

The county seat, Ionia, was twelve miles from my grandfather's cabin. He had to travel on foot and carry what he purchased home in a backpack.

One evening he said to grandmother, "Are there any things you need from the store? I have to go in tomorrow for business. I also need some small articles for the barn. If you need anything, make up a list. I am going to start early in the morning. That way, I can easily get back by nightfall."

"Yes, I do need some things. I will make up a list," my grandmother answered.

So they went to bed early. My grandmother got up at dawn to make a hearty breakfast. She had it ready by the time my grandfather got in from milking. She would take care of the milk.

My grandfather put on his heavy shoes, a jacket with big pockets, and his cap. As he reached the door, he stopped. Turning to my grandmother, he said:

"Do you have any cookies I can take to eat on the way?"

I do not blame him for wanting some of these cookies. She was still making them when I was a little girl. They were called "Sugar Cookies." They were large flat cookies, the tops heavily covered with granulated sugar.

"Yes, I do," she answered. "I just baked some fresh yesterday."

My grandfather came back into the cabin. He went over to the heavy crock jar, took out some cookies and stuffed both his pockets full.

"I'll be home by nightfall," he said.

He trudged down the path from the cabin to the road. It was more an Indian trail than a road. A sturdy cart with a heavy team of horses could negotiate it, but not much else.

He came on to this trail and started walking north to Ionia. After about four miles something loomed in front of him. It was a big black bear. As he knew how dangerous bears were, he was very frightened. These bears would often attack a settler and squeeze or hug him to death. (I wonder if that is where a "bear hug" comes from?)

So my grandfather decided not to move. "Maybe if I stand still he might go right on by me," he muttered. "Maybe he'll think I'm a stump or a tree."

But no, the bear kept coming on, closer and closer and closer. Finally he reached my grandfather. The bear lifted his huge arms as if to hug him. He did put his arms around him, but put on no pressure.

"What is he doing?" my grandfather thought. "Whatever is he doing?"

It was soon evident what he was doing. One huge paw crept down my grandfather's side, until it reached his pocket. Out came the cookies broken in chunks.

"Oh, oh!" thought my grandfather. "So that's it! He wants my cookies. I wish I could slip my hand down and pull my pocket open more."

Well, he did, and succeeded also in getting the other pocket open.

As the bear clawed away, he saw that the cookies had fallen to the ground. Suddenly, he bent down to scoop up the broken cookies with his paw.

My grandfather didn't wait any longer. As the bear ate the cookies, my grandfather fled through the trees and into the woods.

When he reached the forest, he looked back. He could see the bear was still eating cookies. He thankfully said to anyone who wanted to listen:

"Thank God for a sweet tooth!"

Grandma's "Bear" Cookies

Preheat oven to 375 degrees.

Sift together: 2½ cups all purpose flour
1½ teaspoons double-acting baking powder
¾ teaspoon salt
1 teaspoon cinnamon or ¼ teaspoon nutmeg

Combine: 1 cup granulated sugar
¾ cup cooking oil (my grandmother used rendered lard she made herself)
Add to this mixture 2 eggs, one at a time, and beat well after each addition, and 1 teaspoon vanilla

Add the sugar mixture to the sifted flour all at once and beat well.

Shape the dough into ½ inch balls. Flatten the balls as thin as you can between lightly floured hands. If you wish, score them in parallel lines with a fork dipped in flour.

Sprinkle with granulated sugar.

Bake about 10 or 11 minutes on a lightly greased baking sheet.

Enjoy, knowing there are no bears around to pick your pockets!

Another Bear Story

MY GRANDFATHER WENT INTO THE COUNTY SEAT EVERY so often to do business. He then picked up supplies they needed. Usually he could leave early and be home by nightfall.

One time he had some business at the county courthouse. He was sure he could not get back the same day. He worried about leaving my grandmother alone.

As he left that morning, he said, "Stay in the back of the cabin so if anyone comes, they won't see you. By all means, don't go to the door for anyone. Understand?"

"I'll be careful. Don't worry about me," she said.

Everything went well all day. My grandmother worked around the cabin. She made butter in the hand churn. From the whey she got from the butter she made cottage cheese over the fireplace. This was tricky because the whey could not be overcooked or the cheese would be tough.

Not having any cooler, she placed the butter and cheese in a basket at the bottom of the well to keep them fresh. When she needed them she would pull up the basket.

After she had gone back into the cabin, she thought she heard a knock. She listened closely. It was repeated. She hesitated about doing anything. Finally she decided to see who it was.

When she opened the door there stood a foot traveler. He looked dirty, tired and hungry.

"Lady," he said, "could you spare me something to eat and some water? I've traveled a long way and must stop for the night. Do you have a place I can sleep tonight?"

Grandma hesitated. If she fed him he would linger. What she wanted most was for him to be on his way. But her good heart got the best of her.

"If you sit here on the doorstep, I'll bring you something to eat." There was no way she was going to let him in the cabin. "You can wash up at the well and get a drink," she said as she handed him a towel.

At the well there was a handmade bench with a tin water dipper and a washbasin. He pumped some water into it. He used some of the lye soap my grandmother had made. It was strong but it sure cut the dirt.

After he had eaten, my grandmother said, "If you want to, you can sleep in the loft of the barn down by the road. There is fresh hay there and you will be comfortable and warm. There is a ladder on the inside that leads to the loft."

Almost as soon as it was dark my grandmother

went to bed. This was usual because she was up at dawn. Also, the oil lamps did not furnish enough light for any work.

Everything went fine until about 11:00 P.M. She was awakened by the loud noise of men's voices, horses whinnying and the clatter of their hooves. She decided to get up just to take a look.

By the light of some lanterns and a very bright moon, she could make out movement of horses and men and hear loud voices. They seemed to be arguing about something.

"Oh my!" she thought. "I hope that man in the loft keeps quiet." These groups of marauders were dangerous.

After a while, they seemed to settle down. They had evidently gone into the barn for the night. She could still hear their voices raised in loud argument.

Meanwhile, down at the barn things were not going very well. The men could not seem to agree. They were making plans for some raids for the next day.

The man in the loft had heard them come in from the road. He lay very still hoping they would not discover him. He could hear them making their plans and it frightened him. He was in trouble. From stirring up the fresh hay, he had also stirred up the dust.

"Ker-choo! Ker-choo!" he sneezed loudly.

The men below froze into silence.

"What was that?" one of the men said.

"It came from the loft," another answered.

"We'd better look."

"Charles," one of the men said, "get up there and

see what's there."

"I'll do just that," Charles answered as he clumsily went up the homemade ladder.

When he got to the loft he scuffled around. He looked carefully but saw nothing. Then he noticed a movement, so he reached over and tossed the hay back. Cowering there was the traveler.

Charles rushed over and grabbed him by the scruff of the neck. He threw him toward the front of the barn near the ladder.

"There's someone here all right. I'll start him down the ladder and you grab him when he gets down."

When the traveler reached the floor of the barn, the men threw him up against the wall and demanded to know who he was.

He was so frightened he just shook and stared. Not a word came out.

"What are we going to do with him? He heard our plans."

"I don't want to kill him," said the leader. "Let's see what we can find outside."

Soon he came back and said, "I've found just the thing. There's a large barrel outside with a very tight lid. We can put him in there for the night. He can't get out to bother us. We'll be gone by morning before he can raise an alarm."

They pushed him outside and thrust him into the barrel feet first. Someone found a stone and they hammered the lid down tight.

The men then went back into the barn and settled down for the night. They threw themselves down on the ground and using their saddles for pillows were soon asleep.

Meanwhile, in the barrel, the traveler finally stopped shaking. He took stock of his surroundings.

"Although I don't know if I'll ever get out of this barrel, at least I'm alive," he muttered to himself. "Look, here is a large round hole and I can get enough fresh air."

He settled down and had just decided to go to sleep, when he heard footsteps going around and around the barrel. It was more like a shuffle than a step. At last he realized it was a bear. He thought, "At least I am safe from him."

The bear kept going around the barrel, sniffing, sniffing, sniffing. He knew someone was in there and he did not want to give up. Around and around the barrel he went.

Inside the barrel, the traveler kept still. Because of his cramped position, his hands were at the level of the hole. Suddenly, he felt something tickle his finger. He realized it must be the tail of the bear. He kept his hands near the hole and soon it came through the hole again. Grabbing the tail with both hands, he held on with all his strength.

Outside, the bear was startled when his tail disappeared. He decided to take to the woods as fast as he could.

He took off — barrel and all.

The barrel bumped against him. It bounced from tree to tree.

The traveler felt the jolt each time the barrel hit a trunk. He also felt the barrel staves were weakening. Finally, the barrel hit a large tree and fell apart.

The bear did not stop to see what had been in the barrel. He took off through the woods.

The traveler got up and dusted himself off. He found a hollow log in which he spent the rest of the night. In the morning, he returned to the barn to get his belongings. He went up to the cabin to tell my grandmother what had happened and to thank her. He then went on down the trail and on his way.

When my grandfather returned, he was surprised that he had missed so much excitement. He found the parts of the barrel. He took them back to the barn, where I am sure he found some use for them.

Applebutter Days

THERE WERE TWO BIG OCCASIONS WHEN EVERYONE —
family, friends, and neighbors got together at
Grandpa's

One was when they made applebutter. The other
was when they butchered.

The same big black kettle was used for both.

In the Fall, when the apples are ready, calls are
made to everyone about the date for the applebutter
making.

As soon as he had the cabin up, Grandpa had
planted a grove of apple trees along the side by the
road. He had a variety of kinds. I remember two
especially: Snow-apples and Northern Spies. It has
been many years since I have heard of either of
these.

People brought their own knives and jars to
store their applebutter in. Some people brought
their own apples.

The women with their big aprons sat around
hand-hewn tables to prepare apples. The apples

were first washed in big tubs, the stems removed and quartered. Windfalls could be used if they were carefully checked. There were no insecticides so some could be wormy. On the whole, nature pretty well balanced the bug situation. The chickens kept most under control.

The children even helped. In between playing with cousins and friends, they did errands for their elders. They also helped take care of the smaller children. When the cans of discarded apple parts were full, they emptied them into the pigs' swill barrels.

While the women and children worked, the men got the fire started under the big kettle. It took a long time to heat up. It had to be very hot to cook the apples and ingredients.

The best apples were Jonathon or Winesaps. A well-flavored apple got the best results.

The apples were cooked slowly in water, cider or cider-vinegar. The cider base was the best. This

Apple Butter Paddles and Stirrers

Apple or sassafras heads

had to be stirred all the time so it didn't scorch on the bottom. Some folks lined the bottom of the kettle with silver dollars so the pulp would not scorch. The men took turns using big wooden paddles. These paddles were hand-hewn from a piece of timber. They were shaped like a boat oar but with a little wider blade. It had a long handle. Holes were made in the paddle so the pulp would seep through.

Some folks put this through a strainer and returned it to the kettle to finish. Grandpa thought if it was stirred for a long time, this was not necessary.

To this pulp, sugar was added. I suppose someone had figured out the amount. Honey could also be used, as most farmers had bees.

To this was added the seasonings: cinnamon, cloves and allspice. Where Grandma got these I don't know. A few imported things might have been available. Lemon rind and juice could be added if you had it.

This fruit butter was cooked over a low heat, stirring constantly to dissolve the sugar. It was "sheets" cooked, stirring frequently, until the mixture "sheets" from a large wooden spoon. It could also be tested on a plate. When no rim of liquid separated around the edge of the butter, it was done. Grandma was an expert on knowing when it was ready.

It was then poured into hot sterilized jars people had brought. While these were still hot, they would be sealed. Paraffin was used by most, but some had jars with lids that sealed.

These were cooled and stored in a cool, dry place.

This process took all day. At noon, they all took a

break for a big feast; everyone had brought good things to eat from home. The men took turns stirring the kettle while the others ate. It was really a gala event.

During the day, the children played, the ladies gossiped, and the men smoked their pipes and told tall tales.

Everyone helped with the clean-up after, especially the children. We all thought we were "put upon." Then we would get to thinking about that apple butter on a slice of hot fresh bread and realized it was all worth it.

Folks left in early afternoon, as most farmers had cows to milk and cattle to feed.

All of us said: "Hurrah to Applebutter Days!"

an Apple butter pot

an Apple butter paddle

Applebutter Recipe

Jonathan and Winesap apples give best results.

Wash, remove the stems and quarter:	about 4 pounds of apples
Cook slowly until soft in:	2 cups water, cider or cider vinegar

Put fruit through a fine strainer. (My grandparents omitted this.)

For each cup of pulp, add:	½ cup sugar
	3 teaspoons cinnamon
	½ teaspoon cloves
	½ teaspoon allspice

(You may also add grated lemon rind and juice.)

Cook the fruit butter over low heat, stirring constantly until the sugar is dissolved. Continue to cook, stirring once in a while until the mixture sheets from a spoon. You can also place a small quantity on a plate. When no rim of liquids separates around the edge of the butter, it is done.

Pour into hot sterilized jars. Cool on a metal rack or folded dry cloth.

Store in a cool dry place.

*This makes about 5 pints.

Butchering Time

ANOTHER BIG EVENT WHEN THE FAMILY AND FRIENDS got together was butchering time.

As soon as the cabin was up, Grandpa got two young shoats. He kept them close to the cabin to watch them. From these two, he started his piggery.

When a hog got large enough, he would plan a butchering and meat cutting day. This was usually in the Fall when the air was crisp. Late October or early November was a good time.

Families and friends would come in the morning. A large black kettle would be gotten out and a fire started under it. They needed the water boiling. While this was heating, the men would kill the hog down near the barn and bring it up to the yard. Tables were set up like the way they were at apple-butter time.

The carcass was strung up on the branch of a tree or a scaffold built for that. The hog was cut from throat to tail. It was spread open and washed out with water. Men brought pails of cool water from the well and slushed it out.

The insides were then taken out. The liver, heart, kidneys and tongue were given to the women. They placed these in cold water and cleaned them. These items would be given to various members of the families to take home if they wished.

The entrails were carefully removed. These were turned inside out and thoroughly washed. The casings would be used to stuff sausages. Usually there weren't enough of these, so some sausages were salted down in jars or smoked. This process must be done at once.

The men checked the kettle often. When it came to a boil, the carcass was dunked up and down in the boiling water. It was then taken out and put on a table. The men all rushed in to scrape off the hair and bristles. It must be completely free of bristles. Unlike beef cattle the skin of the hog is left on.

First the feet were cut off. These would become pickled pig's feet, a real delicacy. Then the head was severed. Almost all of this would be made into head-cheese. This would also be put down in crocks.

The only thing that was not eaten was the tail, and even then that was also sometimes pickled. Nothing was ever wasted.

The hog itself was then carved up into roasts, ribs, chops, et cetera. The hams were cut ready for smoking.

Some of the parts would be rendered in a hot kettle. This lard was used for cooking and "putting down meat." This meant the meat would be cooked and then packed down in lard in large jars and stored in a cool place.

This was an all day affair. At noon they gathered around the big table for all the goodies the folk had brought.

After the hog was cut up, in the afternoon, the children helped to clean up. Then and then only, could everyone sit down and visit.

Close to early evening, everyone packed their baskets with the pieces of meat they were taking home and ambled on out.

All in all, we had a good time. We all hollered our goodbyes as the horses, buggies and wagons moseyed out of the yard.

Making Country Sausage

At butchering time the popular man was the one who knew how to flavor the sausage, not too much pepper or sage, and just enough coriander.

The uncooked sausage could not be tasted to correct the seasoning and spices. The strength of spices varied so that it was different each time.

There were two ways you could handle this. Play it by ear and hope to have gotten the seasoning right. The best way to learn is to mix a small batch and cook up samples for hungry tasters to test.

At first, the pioneers stuffed the sausage by hand, with the women and children doing most of the work. Later, sausage stuffers were invented which made the work easier and faster. This press had a hand crank. Sausage was put in the top. The casings were stretched over the outlet on the bottom. When the handle was turned, the sausage was pressed into the casing.

Country Sausage

To each part lard use 2 parts of ground pork.
Season this mixture with: thyme
sage
summer savory
coriander
sweet marjoram
pulverized bay leaf
freshly ground pepper
salt

Cook the patties; start them in a cold ungreased pan over moderate heat to suit your taste.

When making this sausage, use it up immediately.

Head Cheese or Brawn

A well-liked old-fashioned dish.

Quarter: a hog's head
Clean teeth, eyes, snout and most of the fat. Soak the quarters about 6 hours in cold water to extract the blood.

Wash the quarters.

Cover with cold water.

Add: 2 onions
5 celery stalks
(Grandma didn't have these. Other seasonings could be used.)

Simmer until the meat is ready to fall from the bones, and dice. Cover it with the stock. Remove the brains.

Add: Salt, pepper, herbs.

Cook for ½ hour. Pour into a mold and cover with a cloth.

Serve, cut into slices. You can serve this with French dressing to which the diced brains have been added.

If you are fortunate enough to live in a very cold climate, which freezes during the winter months, you can prepare head cheese the traditional way. Bury it in a well-prepared hole, lined with gunny sacking, and leave it in the ground all winter. When the Spring thaw comes, you unearth the brawn. The Winter freezing process leaves the meat particularly succulent.

Keeper of the Bees

"**T**HEY'RE SWARMING! THEY'RE SWARMING!"

That was the call I always dreaded when Grandma and I were alone and Grandpa was gone or was in a back field.

One of the first things Grandpa got when he settled in Michigan was a swarm of bees. He got it from another settler whose hives had increased. Sometimes a swarm of wild bees would come in and you could catch them. Also a swarm sometimes got away from its master and flew to a neighbor.

After the hives were built, Grandpa made frames to fit inside. When the bees returned to the hives they would make honey in the honeycomb they formed for storage. These honeycombs were hexagonal wax cells.

Some of the honey would be left in these combs to be eaten that way. Some would be strained out and stored in jars. It did not matter which kind it was, it was delicious on homemade bread or hot biscuits.

Grandma used honey in place of sugar whenever she could. This meant she had to buy less sugar.

My grandfather said there was nothing more thrilling to a beginning beekeeper than the sight of his first hive in the act of swarming.

"They're swarming! They're swarming!" we heard him cry.

The little creatures would rush in frantic haste from the hive like a living stream, filling the air with more and more thousands of bees on the wing.

The worker bees returning from the fields with nectar were carried away by the excitement. They did not even stop to unload their burden in the old hive. They joined the moving bees, tumbling over each other in the mad rush.

Soon the queen bee appeared to take her place among them. She would take her children to a new home. It would be a hive if one was ready. If not, they would find a place of their own. In this case, you might lose the swarm. Sometimes they traveled many miles away from home if not caught.

After the queen joined the swarm, they closed up in a cluster on the branch of a small tree or a bush near the ground.

At this stage of the swarming, the beekeeper took his skep, held it under the swarm, and shook the bees into it.

They then could be transferred into a hive all ready for their return. This is why you had to be prepared. Grandpa usually knew when it was about time and stayed close.

Beekeepers are nervous about their bees. Crowding causes swarming. A thoughtful beekeeper, or bee master as he is often called, can avoid undesired swarming by giving room ahead of time. When the swarming starts, it is almost impossible to control. When the frames get full of honey and there is overcrowding, all the bees can do is move to a new place.

But once in awhile, Grandma and I got caught with the job. Grandma was not as good as Grandpa, but she could do it. The main trouble would be if the bees got settled down on a branch or bush too high for us to reach.

Grandpa loved his bees and I knew they loved him. You should have seen him working with them. I have seen him completely covered with bees and never stung once.

He appreciated "bee craft," as he called it. It was a good open air life, which gave him both health and contentment.

When it came time to take the filled combs from the hive, he usually used a smoker. The smoke is blown into the hive. This alarms the bees so the beekeeper can handle the frames of comb easily and with little trouble. Before Grandpa disturbed the bees, he had another empty hive ready nearby. Thus the bees would not become alarmed by their food supply being taken away.

The smoker was invented by T. F. Bingham of Farwell, Michigan. It is the one most used in the United States and the United Kingdom.

Grandpa wore a bee-veil of fine black net over a broad-brimmed straw hat to protect his face. Sometimes he wore gloves. You must work slowly and

calmly and not resent an occasional sting. To kill a
bee that has stung you is unforgivable.

Vocabulary

Apiary	A place in which a colony or colonies of bees are kept.
Beekeeper	A person who keeps bees.
Beekeeping	The cultivation of the honey bee as a source of food which has existed since ancient times.
Bee Master	Same as beekeeper.
Bee Plants	Any plant used by bees as a source of nectar. White Dutch or common clover is the most important honey producing plant.
Bee Tree	A hollow tree used by wild bees as a hive.
Colony	A group of bees living close together.
Drones	Stingless male bees who make no honey.
Forage	To seek nectar.
Frames	Box-like structures of various shapes for the bees to store their honey.
Hive	A home for bees.
Hived	A body of bees living in a bee hive.

Honeycomb	A structure of rooms of hexagonal wax-cells formed by bees in their hives for the storage of honey.
Nectar	The sweet secretion of a plant which attracts bees.
Pollen	The fertilizing part of flowering plants, usually fine powdery yellowish grains or spores.
Queen Bee	A fertile female bee.
Skep	A round farm basket of wicker or wood. Also a beehive of straw.
Smoker	An appliance with a bellows for blowing smoke into a hive.
Swarm	A body of bees settled together.
Swarming	A body of bees moving forth in great numbers.
Workers	Do the entire labor of a colony.

Feathers

GRANDPA WAS A GOOD FARMER. HIS FARM PROSPERED. Eight children were born to he and my grandmother, of which only four survived. Infant deaths were very high in those days. Usually there was only a rural doctor for quite a large area. They did make house calls, I remember. They always used a horse and buggy. But these visits were few and far between.

The new medicines we have today were not available. Many people died due to this lack. Today they would have probably recovered.

My mother was the only girl that lived. When she was 21 years old she married my father. That was in 1901.

In 1903, my brother, Charles, was born. He was the first grandchild. Everyone doted on him. I am sure he was spoiled but my mother said he was not. He was very intelligent and learned things early. I can remember my mother saying that at age three he could say, "Hipp O Pot A Mus." That evidently was remarkable.

For some reason I never could discover, he was afraid of feathers. He must have had an unhappy experience with something with feathers or fur. Maybe a big rooster. Maybe a raccoon. They were so plentiful in that area at that time.

Whatever the reason, he was afraid. My mother told me often that if she did not want him to go near or on something, she put a feather on it. He would really detour around it.

Charles was my Grandpa's favorite. Grandpa took him along whenever he could.

This one day Grandpa was going to the back field with the team to harrow. As my parents and Charles were there at the time, he asked my mother, "Can I take Charles with me to the back field this morning?"

My mother thought and then said, "I would rather you didn't. It's dangerous near the horses and the machinery. He'd better not go."

"I won't let him near the horses. I'll have him play along the edge of the field or under the big tree back there."

"Oh, all right, if you are careful. You won't be gone too long will you?"

"Only about two hours. We'll be back for lunch."

Off they went to the back field. Charles rode up on the harrow seat on my Grandpa's lap. He held on to him very tightly. Of course, Rover, the big farm dog went along. Grandpa thought Charles would probably play with him. At least the dog could keep an eye on him.

When they got to the field, Grandpa lifted Charles down and put him under the tree. He said to him, "Now you stay right around the tree. You can play on the edge of the field but don't come near the horses where I am working. Rover will be here with you. If you want anything just holler. I'll be near enough so you can see me all the time."

"All right, Grandpa," Charles said. "Rover and I will stay close to the tree."

Grandpa picked up the reins and started to harrow up the field. His crop in this field had been harvested.

The harrow had spike-like teeth which broke up the clods of dirt left after the crop was harvested. Now Grandpa wanted to plant buck wheat. When this was grown and before winter, he would plow it under. It was excellent fertilizer for the soil.

He went around and around the field. The ground was moist. It was easy work for the horses. He kept looking up to see if Charles was all right.

Then when his back was turned as he went around a corner, he heard a loud yell of terror from Charles.

He spun around in his seat and looked toward the tree. He saw that Charles had fallen over and that Rover was chasing a raccoon across the field and into the woods.

Grandpa whipped the horses up and drove as fast as they would go. When he reached the tree, he picked Charles up. He was unconscious and stiff, but he was breathing.

Catching up the reins, Grandpa jumped on the seat and drove to the house. He held Charles closely. He was so glad he had left the gates open.

He drove clear up to the house and just dropped the reins. With Charles in his arms, he ran into the house, calling, "Mother! Mother!" That's what he called Grandma.

Both my mother and Grandma hurried into the kitchen where Grandpa stood still holding Charles, stiff and unconscious.

They put Charles to bed and called the doctor. He came as soon as he could, but he had nine miles to drive with the horse and buggy.

When he arrived, the horse was all covered with lather. Ray, one of my uncles, unhitched her. He took her to the barn for rub-down and cool-off.

Inside the house, the doctor examined Charles, who was still unconscious. The doctor said, "It looks like he's had a convulsion but I can't be sure. It also looks like spinal meningitis. We'll keep him quiet. Bathes him in cool water. We'll see what morning brings. I can't do any more for him."

Of course the doctor could not be sure. There were no laboratories to take tests like we have today. There were no hospitals or clinics for diagnosis. It all depended on the doctor's judgment.

When the doctor returned the next morning, Charles was still unconscious. Within 48 hours of what happened in the field, he was dead.

The doctor's final diagnosis was meningitis. But my mother never agreed. She was sure that the raccoon fell out of the tree where Charles was playing.

He must have brushed by him as he fell. Knowing Charles's fear of fur or feather, she always maintained he had been scared to death.

Cure

WHEN I DID NOT MIND MY FATHER, I ALWAYS SEEMED to end up in trouble and this was no exception.

My grandpa decided to tear down an old shed and build a larger one. As my father was a contractor, he was hired for the job.

"Now you stay away from the area where we are working. We will be tearing down these old timbers. They are rotten and full of rusty nails — large rusty nails. They will be strewn over the ground until we can clean up. It will be very dangerous to be in the area."

"All right, Daddy. I won't. May I just go down to the chicken coop and look up?"

"Yes, just so you do not go any farther."

The men started the wrecking right away. It was so fascinating to me. I sneaked down to the edge of the chicken coop and watched and watched.

Then I edged up a little closer every day. Finally, I was there. Oh yes! I was there! Down came my foot on a large rusty nail sticking up in a board. It came through my foot and stuck out the top.

I screamed. Dad and the men came running. They had to pull the board off my foot. I was crying wildly in pain and fear.

Dad carried me up to the house. Grandma and Mama heated water and soaked my foot in creosote solution. It was a puncture wound and had closed up. I suppose this only sterilized the outer edges. They could only hope that I did not develop blood poisoning or lock-jaw. They did not have tetanus shots or modern medicines to treat infections in those days.

The doctor was called and he came to the house.

"You have done all you can," he said. "Keep her as quiet as possible. I will keep in touch."

It did not do any good. Almost at once I developed blood poisoning. The foot started to inflame and swell. It crept up my leg. They did the only thing they knew: kept some kind of dressing on it.

The leg became so bad that the doctor finally said: "I am sorry. I can do no more. If the infection keeps creeping up the leg, I am afraid we will lose her."

At this stage my Grandfather stepped forward.

"Are you folks all done? If so, I am going to take over. The rest of you stay out of my way and do as I say."

"Mother, said Grandpa, meaning Grandma, "find two large clean pieces of oilcloth. Put one under her, especially the leg area. Give me the other."

With these words he left the room.

Grandma and Mama came in and carefully placed an oilcloth under my leg and upper body.

My mother said, "I wonder what he is going to do?"

"Haven't an idea," Grandma answered.

We soon found out. Grandpa had taken the other oilcloth out to the barn. Meanwhile, he had fastened the cows in their stanchions instead of turning them out. He sat there on a milking stool and watched the cows. When he got an idea a cow was going to go to the bathroom, he ran over, placed a piece of oilcloth under her tail, and caught the warm manure. He then closed it up tight.

Rushing to the house, he ran up the stairs to the bedroom and threw back the covers. He opened the oilcloth and carefully packed the warm manure on and around the leg. Then he covered the leg with the oil cloth and bed covers.

"Keep this on as long as it is warm. I will be back with more a little later."

They kept this up for a day and a night, always changing the poltice when it cooled off.

By the second day you could see the improvement. The pain had eased, the fever was down, and the swelling. The red streak had stopped traveling up my body.

Then they only put the poultice on three or four times a day.

By the fourth day, they discontinued it.

The doctor, meanwhile, had called. He could not believe it. Neither could he explain what had happened.

The leg improved rapidly and I was soon up and around.

Grandpa merely mused and kept his counsel.

My Grandmother always maintained that she never got the smell out of that bedroom. *And*, that was her best bedroom.

Postlude

I have talked to many doctors and bacteriologists about the healing powers of the warm manure. Of course, they could not explain anything. In fact, I do not think they even believed me.

Recently I was talking with a woman who lived many years on a ranch here in the Point Reyes area. I told her about this incident. I was surprised to hear her say: "I believe you. I remember the men would often develop an infection on their fingers, hands or arms that they could not cure. I have seen them go out to the hot manure pile and stick their arm into it and hold it there. It never failed to heal."

I am a firm believer that somewhere in that "cow pie" was a natural antibiotic.

Mind?

WONDER WHY I WOULDN'T MIND? ALMOST EVERY TIME I didn't, I was sorry.

When Grandma first started taking care of the milk, she put it in large earthen crocks. Grandpa would bring it up warm from the barn. It soon cooled off in these jars.

Grandma let it stand until all the cream had come to the top. Then she took a ladle and dipped the cream into a smaller jar.

The skimmed milk stayed in the large jar. It was dipped out of there for various uses. Grandpa used a lot of it to feed his pigs. Grandma let it thicken and fed it to her chickens. Grandpa fed some to his little calves when he had any.

When the cream thickened up, Grandma made butter. At first she had a churn with a dasher. She would sit and work this dasher up and down until the butter "came." You had to know just the right time. She watched it closely near the end. One minute it was just thick cream. The next, small lumps started coming. When these lumps became bigger you were done.

Grandma then drained the butter milk off the butter. She put the butter in a bowl and using a wooden paddle, worked and shaped it up. Sometimes she made big rolls to sell or trade. She even put fancy designs on the top. In those days, you could trade your butter, cheese, and eggs for items at the grocery store.

It was delicious, especially on hot homemade bread. Grandma had to bake all her own bread. There were no bakeries in those days. In fact, the first bakeries I remember were in the 1920s.

The buttermilk left from the churning was also used. They drank a lot of it. What was left was also fed to the chickens and pigs.

Later, Grandma got a milk separator. It was in a small room off the kitchen porch. Grandpa would carry the milk up from the barn in milk pails to this room. Either he or Grandma would run it through the separator.

The milk was poured into a large container at the top. By some magic I did not understand, the skimmed milk went out one spout into a milk can. The cream went through another spout into a container.

This separator was always a fascination to me. In the mechanism, there were cog wheels that turned the machinery. I often watched Grandma run it through. She was always saying to me:

"Now don't you come in here by yourself. You stay away from the separator. You might get hurt."

"All right, Grandma, I won't."

But did I mind? One day when no one was around, I sneaked into that room to play with the separator. I turned the handle and the cogs went around. I kept it up. Then something happened. I wasn't watching what I was doing. My ring finger on my left hand got caught between the cogs. I screamed in pain. Grandma came running. She got my finger out. But the whole end of my finger was practically chewed off.

They took me to the Doctor. He said my finger would heal but the bone and cartilege were all chewed up. To this day you can see the cog marks. (Look, I'll show you.)

I paid dearly for that accident. I could never put any pressure on that finger. I had wanted to be a cellist. I took lessons and got just so far. Because my finger could not exert enough pressure against the heavy strings, I had to give it up.

Why don't we ever learn? That experience should have taught me a lesson.

I remembered just as long as the next time.

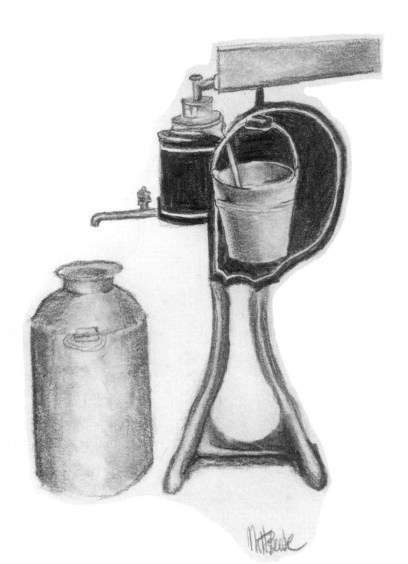

Memories

ISUPPOSE YOU COULD CALL IT A HAUNTED HOUSE BECAUSE every so often I haunted it.

My grandfather built it in the late 1800s. He had lived in a log cabin until that time. Because he was a good farmer, he was able to build a more affluent house by 1900. It was in this spacious, comfortable house that I spent the most enjoyable days of my life.

At regular intervals now, I wander through the rooms and visit every piece of furniture and every nook and cranny. It has been my dearest wish to buy this estate and finish my years out there.

It was an immense house. There were eleven rooms in it, two of which were as large as some peoples' whole house. These were the living room and the bedroom above it. My grandmother always lamented that it was built after her large family was grown and gone away. But maybe that was redeemed by the many hours my family spent there.

The heart of the house was the kitchen. You entered it from a large side porch. When you opened the door, your eyes were immediately drawn to the kitchen stove. If the kitchen was the heart of the house, the stove was the heart of the kitchen. It not only cooked all the food, it also heated that end of the house.

It had everything a stove could have in those days. It was fired with wood. At one end was a reservoir in which Grandma heated water. This was a luxury. Water was obtained from the washroom off the kitchen. It was drawn by a hand pump from the rain cistern beneath the house. Water was carried by pails to the stove.

This stove also had a large baking oven and two warming ovens above the stove proper. It was a treat to get warm home-made bread from one of these. Grandma often put a cast-iron pot on the back of the stove and left it there all day to slowly cook something for supper, which was the evening meal.

The other piece of furniture that dominated the room was a large table. It was pushed into one corner with chairs behind and all around it. Usually only one corner was used — three or four chairs. On this table were many interesting articles. Shining crystal cut-glass cruets held items such as vinegar, salt and pepper shakers, spoons of various sizes and napkins.

I remember Grandma, Grandpa and me sitting in these three chairs for meals. They were always silent meals. We ate and did not talk. I was often scolded by someone saying "eat — don't talk." The saying, "Children are to be seen and not heard," was closely observed in those days.

This table was covered with an oilcloth which usually had a decorative pattern in it. It was easy to keep clean. My grandmother must have had fine linens but I do not remember them. I suppose it was safer to use the oilcloth with so many children at the table.

Over the table was a shelf with a beautiful striking clock. This clock always fascinated me because of the musical tone of its chimes. It must have been expensive even for those days.

To the right of this table was the telephone which

hung on the wall. The saddest memory I have was when I heard my Grandma call my mother to tell her not to bother to buy the shoes she had asked her to. She said she would not need them. I am sure she had a premonition that she would be dead within a week. I felt that depression even as she called. As a child I was psychic to moods in people, especially those I was close to, like my grandmother.

To the left of the room was a magnificent buffet. It was so large it covered almost half of one side wall. It had Grandma's most choice china articles on top. In the bottom was her fine china for setting the table. Maybe her best linens were kept in the bottom drawers.

Next to this on a side wall was a portable tea table. Her water pitchers and drinking glasses were kept here with a good teapot on the lower shelf. I never saw this table moved or used. I wonder why my grandmother had it?

Between the side-board and the tea table was a child's highchair. It always seemed to be in use. There were numerous grandchildren.

Now I often go up those steps on the porch, open the door, go into the washroom to hang up my coat. Here I wash my hands and wipe them on a large linen towel on a roller on the wall. Everyone used this towel. It was hard sometimes to find a dry spot. Then I go past the full woodbox into the kitchen and up to the stove. I lift a lid to see what's cooking. From there I go to the pantry to get a glass of milk and some home-made cookies. I sit down at the table opposite the clock and reminisce over my life in this room. It contains my heart. I feel that my life will also soon be a memory.

ABOUT THE AUTHOR

Louisa M. Burger is a teacher, poet, artist,
musician and writer. She is the author of
Driftwood, a book of poems.
These are true tales. The author herself lived
through many of these experiences. The others
were directly related to her from her
grandmother, grandfather, and mother.
She is a graduate of Western Michigan University
at Kalamazoo, and did graduate work at the
University of Michigan, Michigan State College
and the University of Redlands, California.
She was appointed for a three-year term on
the State Curriculum Committee by the
Governor of Michigan.

ABOUT THE ILLUSTRATOR

Matt Beebe, the illustrator, is a fifteen-year-old
high school student from Columbus, Ohio.
Grandpa and Grandma in this book are his great,
great grandparents.

COLOPHON

Second printing.
Designed and produced by Michael Sykes
at Archetype West in Point Reyes Station.
One thousand copies printed by Stuart and Gay Schecter
at Point Reyes Printing Co in the summer of 1991.
The typeface is Aster.